AF487461

Homiletics: The Art and Science of Preaching

By Larry Watts

Homiletics: The Art and Science of Preaching

By Larry Watts

© Publishing Department of the
General Conference

International Missionary Society of
the Seventh Day Adventists, Reform
Movement

Photo by Jasmin Ne on Unsplash

Contents

"But hath in due times manifested his word through preaching which is committed unto me according to the commandment of God our Saviour." Titus 1:3

I. What is Homiletics?

A. It is the art and science of preaching, communication.

> Romans 10:14, "How then shall they call on him in whom they have not believed? and how shall they believe in him of whom they have not heard? and how shall they hear without a preacher?"

B. Communication is more than talking; it is arresting the attention of your audience in order to facilitate the exchange of information.

> Galatians 6:6, "Let him that is taught in the word communicate unto him that teacheth in all good things."

> Revelation 2:7, "He that hath an ear, let him hear what the Spirit saith unto the churches." [2:11, 17, 29; 3:6, 13, 22] (Matthew 11:15; Mark 4:9; Luke 8:8).

> **Communication is** "the act or process of using words, sounds, signs, or behaviors to express or exchange information or to express your ideas, thoughts, feelings, etc., to someone else." http://www.merriam-webster.com/dictionary

> "Men who assume the responsibility of giving to the people the word from the mouth of God, make themselves accountable for the influence they exert

on their hearers. If they are true men of God, they will know that the object of preaching is not to entertain. It is not merely to convey information, nor to convince the intellect." *–Gospel Workers*, p. 152.

"The object of preaching is not alone to convey information, not merely to convince the intellect. The preaching of the word should appeal to the intellect, and should impart knowledge, but it should do more than this. The words of the minister should reach the hearts of the hearers.--Review and Herald, December 22, 1904." *– Testimonies to Ministers and Gospel Workers*, p. 62.

"If the preaching is of an emotional character, it will affect the feelings, but not the heart and conscience. Such preaching results in no lasting good, but it often wins the hearts of the people and calls out their affections for the man who pleases them. They forget that God has said: 'Cease ye from man, whose breath is in his nostrils.' " *–Testimonies for the Church*, vol. 5, o. 301.

C. "Short and sweet" is better than "long and boring."

    1. Bring the Bible to life, and you will not bore the people.

2. Stay on the subject. Do not go off on rabbit trails.
3. More than five main points are too many.
4. "If you have not hit oil in 20 minutes, stop drilling." S. Gutknecht.
5. "Let illustrations be choice [few] rather than numerous." *–Counsels to Writers and Editors*, p. 172.

II. What Is Preaching? Who Is a Preacher?

A. The mouthpiece and messenger of God to the people.

> "Be thou for the people to Godward." Exodus 18:19.

> "The minister stands as God's mouthpiece to the people, and in thought, in word, in act, he is to represent his Lord." *–Gospel Workers*, p. 20.

> "The minister is not infallible, but God has honored him by making him His messenger." *–Testimonies for the Church*, vol. 5, p. 298.

B. It is the most important calling on earth.

> "The highest of all work is ministry in its various lines, and it should be kept before the youth that there is no work

more blessed of God than that of the gospel minister." *–Evangelism*, p. 23.

C. On the other hand, a priest represents the people before the Lord.

> "The priest in the holy place, directing his prayer by faith to the mercy-seat, which he could not see, represents the people of God directing their prayers to Christ before the mercy-seat in the heavenly sanctuary." *–The Spirit of Prophecy*, vol. 1, p. 273. [See also Zechariah 3:1-3.]

D. Full-time ministry is a calling from God.
1. Acts 13:2; Romans 1:1, Separated by Holy Ghost and the church.
2. 2 Timothy 2:4, Not involved in worldly matters (Levites set apart, Lev. 1:50-53.)
3. Philippians 4:14, A supreme vocation
4. 2 Timothy 1:9, A holy calling

III. The Goal of the Preacher Concerning the People

A. It is to see souls transformed into the image of Jesus.

The Lord's glory should be included in every message. 2 Corinthians 3:18, "But we all, with open face beholding as in a glass the glory of the Lord, are changed into the same image from glory to glory, even as by the Spirit of the Lord."

"The salvation of souls is the great object." – *Testimonies for the Church*, vol. 1, p. 442.

The minister is "to use his entire strength in pushing forward the cause of God. His mind should be clear, and centered upon the one object of saving souls." –*Testimonies for the Church*, vol. 4, p. 265.

B. It is to prepare a people to stand complete in the day of the Lord.

Colossians 1:28, "Whom we preach, warning every man, and teaching every man in all wisdom; that we may present every man perfect in Christ Jesus."

"It is true that our warfare is aggressive, but our weapons are to be those found in a plain "Thus saith the Lord." Our work is to prepare a people to stand in the great day of God. We should not be turned aside to lines that will encourage controversy, or arouse antagonism in those not of our faith." – *Counsels to Writers, Teachers, and Editors*, p. 68.

"Our work is not to make a raid on the Government but to prepare a people to stand in the great day of the Lord. The fewer attacks we make on authorities and powers, the more work will we do for God. . . .

"While the truth must be defended, this work is to be done in the spirit of Jesus. If God's people work without peace and love, they work at a great loss, an irretrievable loss. Souls are driven from Christ even after they have been connected with His work." – Evangelism, p. 173.

"Prepare to meet thy God." [Amos 4:12.]

"The fear of the LORD [is] the beginning of wisdom: a good understanding have all they that do [His commandments]: His praise endureth for ever." Psalm 11:10.

Proverbs 4:7, "Wisdom is the principal thing; therefore get wisdom: and with all thy getting get understanding."

What is wisdom?
a. To know.
b. To understand.
c. To apply.
d. To practice.

Knowledge is known information needed to understand a subject, with the potential of using that knowledge for a specific purpose.

Wisdom is the ability to make good decisions based on life's experiences as well as information and knowledge.

C. To lead the people to Christ

Mark 6:34, "And Jesus, when He came out, saw much people, and was moved with compassion toward them, because they were as sheep not having a shepherd: and He began to teach them many things."

1. Jesus said the people need a shepherd.
2. A shepherd is a leader, a guide and protector.

"To neglect or despise those whom God has appointed to bear the responsibilities of leadership in connection with the advancement of the truth, is to reject the means that He has ordained for the help, encouragement, and strength of His people." *–The Acts of the Apostles*, p. 164.

Preaching is one way to guide them.

D. To call sinners to repentance

1 Corinthians 9:16, "For though I preach the gospel, I have nothing to glory of for necessity is laid upon me; yea, woe is unto me, if I preach not the gospel!"

1. Not for an occupation.
2. Not just because one is a good speaker.
3. Not to make money.
4. Not to receive the praise of man.
5. Not because it is an honorable position.
6. Not to be like someone else.
7. Not to cut someone up – make bricks from the word in order to stone the people for their sins.

"Preaching should comfort the disquieted and disquiet the comfortable."

"The preaching of the word is ordained of God to arouse and convict sinners. And when the living preacher exemplifies in his own life the self-denial and sacrifices of Christ, when his conversation and acts are in harmony with the divine Pattern, then his influence will be a powerful one upon those who listen to his voice." –*Testimonies for the Church*, vol. 4, p. 118.

IV. What to Preach

Present the truth as it is in Jesus.

"Ministers need to have a more clear, simple manner in presenting the truth as it is in Jesus. Their own minds need to comprehend the great plan of salvation more fully. Then they can carry the minds of the hearers away from earthly things to the spiritual and eternal....

"Those whose hearts are filled with the love of Jesus, with the precious truths of His Word, will be able to draw from the treasure house of God things new and old. They will not find time to relate anecdotes; they will not strain to become orators, soaring so high that they cannot carry the people with them; but in simple language, with touching earnestness, they will present the truth as it is in Jesus....

"Study the history of God's people. Recount God's past dealings with His people....

"The truth of the ministration of angels.... Do not indulge in fanciful speculations....

"[T]he free gift of Christ's righteousness.... Put Christ into every sermon. Let the preciousness, mercy, and glory of Jesus Christ be dwelt upon; for Christ formed within is the hope of glory." —*Selected Messages*, book. 1, pp. 157, 158

"The disciples were men who knew how to speak and pray sincerely, men who could take hold of the might of the Strength of Israel. ... They could hold forth the word of life because they had received the heavenly anointing. Jesus Christ, the wisdom and power of God, was the theme of every discourse." —*The Acts of the Apostles*, p. 594.

" 'Behold,' said Jesus, 'I send you forth as sheep in the midst of wolves: be ye therefore wise as serpents, and harmless as doves." Christ Himself did not suppress one word of truth, but He spoke it always in love. He exercised the greatest tact, and thoughtful, kind attention in

His intercourse with the people. He was never rude, never needlessly spoke a severe word, never gave needless pain to a sensitive soul. He did not censure human weakness. He fearlessly denounced hypocrisy, unbelief, and iniquity, but tears were in His voice as He uttered His scathing rebukes...." –*The Desire of Ages*, p. 353.

V How to Preach

A. Not with man's wisdom, but by God's power

1. Let self fade away. Glory in God.

   2 Corinthians 10:17, 18, "But he that glorieth, let him glory in the Lord. For not he that commendeth himself is approved, but whom the Lord commendeth."

   1 Corinthians 2:4, 5, "And my speech and my preaching was not with enticing words of man's wisdom, but in demonstration of the Spirit and of power That your faith should not stand in the wisdom of men, but in the power of God."

2. Speak in the common man's language, not with enticing words.

   "In beautiful language and with a musical voice he told of the words and works of Christ, speaking in a way that impressed the hearts of those who heard him. The simplicity of his words, the sublime power of the truths he uttered, and the fervor that characterized his teachings, gave him access to all classes." –*The Acts of the Apostles*, p. 546.

3. Have the Holy Ghost's power upon you, and be filled with the Spirit.

> "Ministers must seek God for His Holy Spirit, in order that they may present the truth aright." –*Evangelism*, p. 91.

B. Presenting the Holy Spirit's message

1 Corinthians 2:13, "Which things also we speak, not in the words which man's wisdom teacheth, but which the Holy Ghost teacheth; comparing spiritual things with spiritual."

Spirit filled preaching...

1. Sometimes brings success. Example—3000 baptized at Pentecost.
2. Sometimes it brings death. Example—Stephen & John the Baptist.
3. Sometimes it leads to exile or prison. Example—John, Paul and Silas.
4. We are to do the right and leave the results with God, both for ourselves and for the hearers.

2 Corinthians 2:16, "To the one [we are] the savour of death unto death; and to the other the savour of life unto life. And who [is] sufficient for these things?"

"In our lifework we know not which shall prosper, this or that. This is not a question for us to settle. We are to do our work, and leave the results with God. 'In the morning sow thy seed, and in the evening withhold not thine hand.' Ecclesiastes 11:6." –*Evangelism*, p. 490.

VI. To Get A Message – Ask these questions

A. Has the message come from God by my communion with the Holy Spirit?

Ask the Holy Spirit for a message. Luke 11:9-13, "And I say unto you, Ask, and it shall be given you; seek, and ye shall find; knock, and it shall be opened unto you.... If ye then, being evil, know how to give good gifts unto your children: how much more shall [your] heavenly Father give the Holy Spirit to them that ask Him?"

B. Have I prayed fervently and asked specifically for the sermon?

James 4:2, "Ye have not, because ye ask not."

C. Have I used common sense?

What do the people need at this time?

Colossians 3:17, "Whatsoever ye do in word or deed, do all in the name of the Lord Jesus, giving thanks to God and the Father by him."

"We are to be guided by true theology and common sense. Our souls are to be surrounded by the atmosphere of heaven." –*Mind, Character and Personality*, vol. 1, p. 146.

1 Timothy 6:20, "O Timothy, keep that which is committed to thy trust, avoiding profane [and] vain babblings, and oppositions of science falsely so called."

"Guard your words. Let sobriety and sound common sense characterize your conversation. Do not trifle with the purity and nobility of your souls by condescending to indulgence in stale jokes, and in cultivating habits of trifling conversation." –*The Youth's Instructor*, May 30, 1895.

D. What can I share of what I have learned from my experience with God?

Acts. 20:35, "[R]emember the words of the Lord Jesus, how He said, It is more blessed to give than to receive."

Matthew 13:52, "Then said He unto them, Therefore every scribe which is instructed unto the kingdom of heaven is like unto a man that is an householder which bringeth forth out of his treasure things new and old."

"[W]hat have you to say for yourselves? What soul conflicts have you experienced that have been for your good, for the good of souls, and for the glory of God?" –*Review and Herald*, December 20, 1881.

E. What can I preach to encourage the people to do right, affirming constantly the same truths?

Titus 3:8, "This is a faithful saying, and these things I will that thou affirm constantly that they which have believed in God might be careful to maintain good works. These things are good and profitable unto men."

"Ministers who labor in word and doctrine should be thorough workmen, and should present the truth in its purity, yet with simplicity. They should feed the flock with clean provender, thoroughly winnowed...

"The truth should be presented in a manner which will make it attractive to the intelligent mind." –*Testimonies for the Church*, vol.1. p. 414.

F. What can I give in the form of milk and meat?

Do not choke the babies on meat: keep it simple. Do not give mature souls just milk. (See 1 Corinthians 2:1-10; Hebrews 5:11-14.)

1 Corinthians 3:2, "I have fed you with milk, and not with meat: for hitherto ye were not able to bear it, neither yet now are ye able."

VII. Types of Sermons

A. Based on a word

Take one word.

Study its meaning. What did it mean to the people who first heard it? Where is it first used? Did its meaning change over time? Share what you have learned about it. For example, where is the Hebrew word "love" first found in scripture? Where is the last place it is found in Greek? What is the real meaning of "charity" (I Corinthians 13)? What words or phrases are used when speaking of deliverance, patience, compassion, sanctification, etc? What personal experiences are associated with these words and concepts?

Isaiah 28:10, "For precept *must be* upon precept, precept upon precept; line upon line, line upon line; here a little, *and* there a little."

B. Based on topics

Pick a topic such as:

1. How to have a happy marriage – family.
2. What do we owe the government? Respect, taxes, involvement, prayer.
3. How to have revival.
4. Successful soul-winning.
5. Getting things through prayer.
6. How to love God, etc.

C. Based on doctrine

1. Soteriology—salvation
2. Theology proper—God
3. Pneumatology—Holy Spirit
4. Christology—Jesus Christ
5. Eschatology—end time events
6. Bibliology—the Bible
7. Angelology—angels, Satan, demons
8. Anthropology—man
9. The miracles of Jesus
10. The parables of Jesus
11. The blood atonement
12. Bodily resurrection, etc.
13. The sanctuary types and shadows
14. The three angels' message

15. Christ Our Righteousness and justification by faith
16. Etc.

D. Based on characters

1. Joseph and the coat of many colors.
2. Rahab, the harlot who saved the spies and her family.
3. Ruth, the Moabites', who came into the lineage of Jesus.
4. Samuel, the last judge of Israel.
5. Eli, the father who did not restrain his children.
6. Reuben, the unstable father.
7. Lot, the backslidden father.
8. One of the Apostles: Peter, James, John, etc.
9. Almost every man and woman in the Bible can be preached on.

E. Based on the books of the Bible

Preach through any one of the 66 books in the Bible, verse by verse, chapter by chapter, or thought by thought.

F. Based on occasions

1. Weddings, funerals
2. New year's messages
3. The marriage in Cana
4. Special messages for holidays (Mother's Day, etc.)
5. Jesus' baptism
6. The day of Pentecost
7. The day of Atonement, etc.

VIII. Types of Preaching

1. "Reprove, rebuke, exhort." 2 Timothy 4:2.

A. reproof—to refute or to expose false teaching and practice

Job 26:11, "The pillars of heaven tremble and are astonished at his reproof."

Proverbs 1:23, "Turn you at my reproof: behold, I will pour out my spirit unto you, I will make known My words unto you."

Proverbs 1 :25, "But ye have set at nought all my counsel, and would none of my reproof."

Proverbs 1:30, "They would none of My counsel: they despised all my reproof."

Proverbs 5:12, "And say, How have I hated instruction, and my heart despised reproof"

Proverbs 10:17, "He is in the way of life that keepeth instruction: but he that refuseth reproof erreth."

Proverbs 12:1, "Whoso loveth instruction loveth knowledge: but he that hateth reproof is brutish."

Proverbs 13:18, "Poverty and shame shall be to him that refuseth instruction: but he that regardeth reproof shall be honoured."

Proverbs 15:5, "A fool despiseth his father's instruction: but he that regardeth reproof is prudent."

Proverbs 15:10, "Correction is grievous unto him that forsaketh the way: and he that hateth reproof shall die."

Proverbs 15:31, 32, "The ear that heareth the reproof of life abideth among the wise. 32 He that refuseth instruction despiseth his own soul: but he that heareth reproof getteth understanding."

Proverbs 17:10, "A reproof entereth more into a wise man than an hundred stripes into a fool."

Proverbs 29:15, "The rod and reproof give wisdom: but a child left to himself bringeth his mother to shame."

2 Timothy 3:16, "All scripture is given by inspiration of God, and is profitable for doctrine, for reproof for correction, for instruction in righteousness:"

B. Rebuke—to scold in love

Proverbs 9:8, "Reprove not a scorner, lest he hate thee: rebuke a wise man, and he will love thee."

Proverbs 13:1 , "A wise son heareth his father's instruction: but a scorner heareth not rebuke."

Proverbs 13:8, "The ransom of a man's life are his riches: but the poor heareth not rebuke."

Proverbs 24:25, "But to them that rebuke him shall be delight, and a good blessing shall come upon them."

Proverbs 27:5, "Open rebuke is better than secret love. "

Ecclesiastes 7:5, "It is better to hear the rebuke of the wise, than for a man to hear the song of fools."

Luke 17:3, "Take heed to yourselves: If thy brother trespass against thee, rebuke him; and if he repent, forgive him."

1 Timothy 5:20, "Them that sin rebuke before all, that others also may fear "

2 Timothy 4:2, "Preach the word; be instant in season, out of season; reprove, rebuke, exhort with all longsuffering and doctrine."

Titus 1 :13, "This witness is true. Wherefore rebuke them sharply that they may be sound in the faith;"

Titus 2:15, "These things speak, and exhort, and rebuke with all authority Let no man despise thee."

C. Exhortation

Interpreted "advocate"—"to run to one's side and pick him up" as in 1 John 2:1, "My little children, these things write I unto you, that ye sin not. And if any man sin, we have an advocate with the Father, Jesus Christ the righteous."

Hebrews 3:13, 14. "But exhort one another daily, while it is called To day; lest any of you be hardened through the deceitfulness of sin. For we are made partakers of Christ, if we hold the beginning of our confidence steadfast unto the end."

2. Help, encourage, assurance, and comfort sermons

1 Thessalonians 4:1, "Furthermore then we beseech you, brethren, and exhort you by the Lord Jesus, that as ye have received of us how ye ought to walk and to please God, so ye would abound more and more."

1 Thessalonians 5:14, "Now we exhort you, brethren, warn them that are unruly, comfort the feebleminded, support the weak, be patient toward all men."

1 Timothy 6:2, "And they that have believing masters, let them not despise them, because they are brethren; but rather do them service, because they are faithful and beloved, partakers of the benefit. These things teach and exhort."

2 Timothy 4:2, "Preach the word be instant in season, out of season; reprove, rebuke, exhort with all longsuffering and doctrine."

Titus 1:9, 'Holding fast the faithful word as he hath been taught that he may be able by sound doctrine both to exhort and to convince the gainsayers. "

Titus 2:6, "Young men likewise exhort to be sober minded."

Titus 2:9, "Exhort servants to be obedient unto their own masters, and to please them well in all things; not answering again."

Titus 2:15, "These things speak, and exhort, and rebuke with all authority. Let no man despise thee."

Hebrews 3:13, "But exhort one another daily while it is called To day; lest any of you be hardened through the deceitfulness of sin."

1 Peter 5:1, "The elders which are among you I exhort, who am also an elder and a witness of the sufferings of Christ, and also a partaker of the glory that shall be revealed:"

D. Devotional, importance of

1. Deals with our personal, intimate relationship to God.
2. Deals with our public worship, communion with God through the Holy Spirit, and seeking the Lord together as a people, and hearing His voice, both individually and collectively.
3. Etc.

E. Exegetical (related to VII.A)

Explanation or interpretation of a Bible word, phrase, verse or passage. It seeks the underlying meaning of the passage from the context of history, original grammar [Hebrew or Greek] along with the belief systems of the time of writing. It then attempts to apply the lessons to today. Exegesis also builds upon hermeneutical principles to breakdown the ideas present so that modern readers can apply the lessons personally. Some claim that expository sermons are "unbiblical" in the sense that the books of the Bible were written to deal with specific issues and topics and that Paul and Peter wrote topically and used "texts" to support their points. However, the truest Spirit-directed exegetical approach is simply one of discovery, seeking to find what the passage really says and means and how it applies to us today – all under the guidance of the Holy Spirit. It has an advantage over the topical approach in that the passage itself provides the topic and therefore one need not keep coming up with an endless number of topics on which to preach.

F. Topical Sermons

A topical message is a sermon in which a preacher uses several passages to support a thesis about a particular topic. (What does the Bible say about ______?) [See section VII.] Topical sermons are similar to Bible Studies and usually use "proof text" methodology.

G. Expository

"The distinguishing mark of expository preaching, also called Bible Exposition, is the biblical interpretation communicated through the sermon. The expositor must teach his audience the meaning of the text intended by its author and understood by its original recipients. Because the original languages of the Old and New Testaments are inaccessible to almost all congregations, precise and detailed interpretations of Scripture will be also. So a Bible expositor's central responsibility is to acquaint them with these interpretations previously unknown to them. The final test of the effectiveness of Bible Exposition is how well individuals who hear the sermon can go home and read the passage with greater comprehension of its exact meaning than they could before they heard the message.... Expose a portion of Scripture. An expository sermon seeks to give the audience the meaning of a text that was intended by its author and what its original recipients should have understood from it. Most conservative churches would argue that expository preaching is the only way to preach." *The Relationship Between Exegesis and Expository Preaching,* Robert L. Thomas [http://www.tms.edu/m/tmsj2i.pdf]

H. Textual – similar to Expository and Topical

A text message used a single Bible passage as a jumping-off point to discuss a particular thesis. (e.g., 1 Corinthians 13 to discuss Love Is an Action). Similar to Topical but centers on a particular passage, whereas Topical uses "proof text method" to support its thesis.

I. Compare and Contrast

The book of Hebrews is a perfect example of this approach to spiritual subjects. Compare and contrast takes two things that are quite similar, usually one physical and the other spiritual, and shows how they are alike and yet different in some very significant ways. Examples are Hagar and Sarah (Gal. 4:22-27); Adam and Christ (Romans 5:12-19); Christ and Melchisedec (Hebrews 7); types and antitypes, etc.

IX. The Sermon

Where to begin

1. Know your audience

    As much as possible, know the congregation to whom you will be speaking. From the very beginning of your preparation, determine to feed them good spiritual food thoroughly winnowed. Inspire them with what has inspired you.

2. Realize the sacredness of the place, the work, and the task.

    Try to think of everything ahead of time. Don't leave anything to chance or the initiative of others. If you are using PowerPoint, make sure all the equipment and adaptors are available and working before the meeting begins. Everyone involved should know what he or she is to do before the meeting begins. Then there will be no confusion or need of talking (or whispering in the front) to give instructions on what to do. Our God is a God of order, not of confusion.

    "System and order are manifest in all the works of God throughout the universe. Order is the law of heaven, and it should be the law of God's people on the earth." –*General Conference Daily Bulletin*, January 29, 1893.

3. Live what you preach and pray

    "The Lord is waiting to manifest through His people His grace and power. But He requires that those who engage in His service shall keep their minds ever directed to Him. Every day they should have time for reading the Word of God and for prayer....

"Individually we are to walk and talk with God; then the sacred influence of the gospel of Christ in all its preciousness will appear in our lives.

"There is an eloquence far more powerful than the eloquence of words in the quiet, consistent life of a pure, true Christian. What a man is has more influence than what he says.

"The officers who were sent to Jesus came back with the report that never man spoke as He spoke. [John 7:46] But the reason for this was that never man lived as He lived. Had His life been other than it was, He could not have spoken as He did. His words bore with them a convincing power, because they came from a heart pure and holy, full of love and sympathy, benevolence and truth.

"It is our own character and experience that determine our influence upon others...." *—God's Amazing Grace*, p. 276.

"He who loves Christ the most will do the greatest amount of good. There is no limit to the usefulness of one who, by putting self aside, makes room for the working of the Holy Spirit upon his heart, and lives a life wholly consecrated to God. If men will endure the necessary discipline, without complaining or fainting by the way, God will teach them hour by hour, and day by day." *—The Desire of Ages*, pp. 250, 251.

4. Leave room for the Holy Spirit's direction

Ephesians 4:30, "And grieve not the Holy Spirit of God, whereby ye are sealed unto the day of redemption."

At first, we may feel the need to have every word written and just read the message, or put everything in the PowerPoint. But following a prepared script leaves no room for the Holy Spirit to work. The art of good PowerPoints is another topic, but suffice it here to say that if they are absolutely necessary, their written content should be limited, otherwise why does the audience need you? And how can you be moved by God in the service? You'er stuck with your presentation.

Psalm 78:40, 41, "How oft did they provoke Him in the wilderness, and grieve him in the desert! Yea, they turned back and tempted God, and limited the Holy One of Israel."

Entering the pulpit [desk]

"When the minister enters, it should be with dignified, solemn mien. He should bow down in silent prayer as soon as he steps into the pulpit, and earnestly ask help of God. What an impression this will make! There will be solemnity and awe upon the people. Their minister is communing with God; he is committing himself to God before he dares to stand before the people. Solemnity rests upon all, and angels of God are brought very near. Every one of the congregation, also, who fears God should with bowed head unite in silent prayer with him that God may grace the meeting with His presence and give power to His truth proclaimed from human lips...." *–Testimonies for the Church*, vol. 5, p. 493.

Each sermon should have three parts:

1. Introduction
2. Body of the message
3. Conclusion / Appeal [CTA: Call To Action]

Another way to say it...

- "...Tell them what you are going to say..."
- "...Then say it..."
- "...Then tell them what you have said."

A. Introduction

The Title

The title of the sermon should not be more spectacular than the sermon. Jesus got right to the point:

"Ye are the light of the world..."
"Ye are the salt of the earth..."
"A sower went forth to sow..."

The title should or could:

- be a signpost to where the sermon is going.
- create curiosity for the rest of the message.
- be a question to be answered.

Scripture reading

"For if the trumpet give an uncertain sound, who shall prepare himself to the battle? So likewise ye, except ye utter by the tongue words easy to be understood, how shall it be known what is spoken? for ye shall speak into the air." 1 Corinthians 14:8, 9.

Some preachers read a text, do not give a title, chase rabbits, say some good things, ramble on, close, and then leave there hearers puzzled. The people wonder, "What was all that about?"

We should go to the other extreme. We should speak in such clear and simple tones that it is not only perfectly understood what we said, but it is impossible to misunderstand what we said. "Seeing then that we have such hope, we use great plainness of speech." 2 Corinthians 3:12.

The Introduction should...

- be an accurate signpost pointing to the sermon.
- create hunger for the rest of the message.
- lead the people to feel that the sermon has answers to individual needs.
- be the most articulate part of the sermon.
- have as its last sentence the vision statement of the message.

Some preachers can build to a climax and have people hang on long enough to get the one point – MOST CANNOT! Others let the cat out of the bag at the beginning, so every one knows everything they are talking about right from the start. Preachers are not to be storytellers. Don't seek to be a great preacher; seek to be a clear preacher. Don't be mystical but crystal clear.

"I charge thee therefore before God, and the Lord Jesus Christ, who shall judge the quick and the dead at His appearing and His kingdom: Preach the word; be instant in season, out of season; reprove, rebuke, exhort with all long-suffering and doctrine." 2 Timothy 4:1, 2.

> "The minister of Christ ... is to 'preach the word,' not the opinions and traditions of men, not pleasing fables or sensational stories, to move the fancy and excite the emotions. He is not to exalt himself, but as in the presence of God he is to stand before a dying world and preach the word. There is to be no levity, no trifling, no fanciful interpretation; the minister must speak in sincerity and deep earnestness, as a voice from God expounding the Sacred Scriptures. He is to bring to his hearers those things which most concern their present and eternal good." —*Gospel Workers*, p. 147.

Four points to consider in the introduction:

1. Read the scriptures clearly. Make sure the scriptures fit your message exactly.
2. It is not improper to say a short public prayer asking God to help the hearers to understand your specific subject.
3. Repeat the title of your message loudly and clearly at least several times during your introduction.
4. The introduction should be brief and well structured.

Do not delay getting into your topic with formalities and announcements. Leave that to others. Remember the time in the pulpit is doubly sacred and belongs to God. Clarity, with simplicity, is the goal:

1 Corinthians 14:10-12, "There are, it may be, so many kinds of voices in the world, and none of them is without signification. Therefore if I know not the meaning of the voice, I shall be unto him that speaketh a barbarian, and he that speaketh shall be a barbarian unto me. Even so ye, forasmuch as ye are zealous of spiritual gifts seek that ye may excel to the edifying of the church."

Ephesians 4:12, 13, "For the perfecting of the saints, for the work of the ministry, for the edifying [building up] of the body of Christ: Till we all come in the unity of the faith, and of the knowledge of the Son of God, unto a perfect man, unto the measure of the stature of the fulness of Christ."

Build up the church; do not confuse the church!

B. The Body of the Sermon

A good sermon is like a good piece of music. It will have real and perceived structure.

The first aspect of the body is to define a skeleton outline related to the text and subject the Holy Spirit has led you to preach on.

- Examples of skeleton outlines include:

1. Pointed message

Some truths we must preach require many points, depending on the subject. These topics are like the Sonata-allegro form of a symphony: At least two contrasting themes are heard in variations throughout the piece.

- How to have a happy family
- How to handle your finances
- How to win souls
- How to interpret scripture
- Steps of man's degeneracy (Romans 1)
- Possibilities of faith, etc.

2. One great truth

Some sermons stress just one great truth, and the same idea is repeated from different points of view, like a theme with variations:

- Duty
- Compassion
- Others
- Commitment

3. Alliterations

Repetitions of the same first letter or sound in a group of words. Examples:

- Titus 2:14 – Salvation, Sanctification, Service
- Philemon's love – Refreshing, Receiving, Reciprocating
- Spirit filled Attitudes – Ephesians 5:18-21-Singing, Satisfaction, Submission

4. Acrostic

Words formed from the first letters of other words.

- FAITH – Forsaking All I Trust Him
- GRACE – God's Riches At Christ's Expense;
  God's Resources At Christian Experiences

5. Verses that outline themselves

Look up in your Bible and notice how easily these verses outline themselves:

- James 3:17
- Titus 2:4, 5
- 2 Chronicles 7:14
- 1 Corinthians 13:4-8

6. Two kinds of outlines

- Alternation: this is also called compare and contrast the outline would look like this:
  - A
    - B
  - A
    - B (or A, B, C; A, B, C, etc.)
- Inversion (or introversion) would look like this:
  - A
    - B
    - B
  - A (or in extended form would be: A, B, C; C, B, A, etc.)

Now that you have an outline, it is time to add some meat to it. Fill in the body of the sermon by using:

1. Definition of terms

    Use a dictionary or concordance to explain terms to the people. Do not presume that they know what words mean. "So they read in the book in the law of God distinctly and gave the sense, and caused them to understand the reading." Nehemiah 8:8.

2. Illustrations
    a. Personal illustrations
    b. Borrowed illustrations from books
    c. People in the Bible who might illustrate the point.
    d. Facts pertaining to the topic from history, science, archaeology, encyclopedia, etc.
    e. Stories that make a point.

3. Poems/Hymns

    An appropriate poem or hymn should fit the point exactly

4. Practical aspects

    Do not let people figure it out; explain it to them. For instance, explain what a "prayer closet" is, what a "minuteman" is, etc.

"His [Jesus'] messages of mercy were varied to suit His audience. He knew 'how to speak a word in season to him that is weary' (Isaiah 50:4); for grace was poured upon His lips, that He might convey to men in the most attractive way the treasures of truth. He had tact to meet the prejudiced minds, and surprise them with illustrations that won their attention. Through the imagination He reached the heart." *—The Desire of Ages*, p. 254.

C. The Conclusion

Remember: tell them what you are going to say (introduction), then say it (the body), and then tell them what you said (conclusion). Take this opportunity to clarify the main message. It would be wise at least to repeat your points.

Also, if something was not clear in the message, try to clear it up briefly. Do not bore people by preaching the whole sermon again; just highlight the main points.

D. Invitation-Appeal

Every message should have a CTA (Call to Action). It is the time to respond to God and His love. The preacher should make that clear. It is the time to apply the truth to our lives. James 1:22, "But be ye doers of the word, and not hearers only, deceiving your own selves."

From the brain to the heart is less than a millisecond, but the truth cannot come into the heart until it is practiced in the life.

Jesus said, "My house shall be called the house of prayer." Matthew 21:13. Ask the hearers to pray about the application of the message. The closing hymn should be the congregation's response to the message.

Appeal to the congregation to give their lives in consecration to God.

X. Pulpit Etiquette

Colossians 4:6, "Let your speech be always with grace, seasoned with salt, that ye may know how ye ought to answer every man."

Luke 4:22, "And all bare Him witness, and wondered at the gracious words which proceeded out of his mouth...."

A. Appearance

    1. Be simple (not something that is excessive).
    2. Be clean (hair clean and cut).
    3. Stand up straight.

B. The pulpit

    1. Do not lean on it.
    2. Do not move it around.
    3. Do not play with it.
    4. If you are short. have a small platform to stand on.
    5. Treat it as the sanctified place that it actually is.
       (Do not worship it, but encourage young and old to respect it.)

C. Microphone

    1. Talk into it.

    2. Have the PA loud enough so people in the back row can hear you speaking at a normal voice level.

    3. Use more treble than bass.

       a. Bass muddles your voice.

       b. Treble allows your voice to be clear.

    4. It is better to be too loud than too soft. (At least you will be heard.)

D. Your eyes

    1. Make eye contact with all the people

    2. Do not look at the same person. Look around.

    3. If you are nervous, look over the top and scan the back.

    4. Look away from distractions and don't give latecomers any attention.

    5. If you are being translated, do not look at the translator unless for effect.

E. Your hands and feet

    1. Do not play with the pulpit.

    2. Do not keep adjusting the microphone.

    3. Do not play with your glasses or tie.

    4. Make appropriate gestures to help illustrate the message.
Example: we serve a "Big God" – spread your arms out.

5. Do not touch your face if at all possible.
6. Shuffle your notes quietly.
7. Don't move back and forth like a tree in the wind.

F. Your voice

1. Speak loudly and clearly.
2. Speak slowly so all can understand you.
3. Preach with emotion—from your heart with love
4. Don't be afraid of silence
5. Do not be a boring preacher!
6. Ask yourself, "How would Jesus present this topic?"

Ephesians 4:15, "But speaking the truth in love, may grow up into Him in all things, which is the head, even Christ:"

1 Corinthians 14:8, "For if the trumpet give an uncertain sound, who shall prepare himself to the battle?"

Isaiah 58:1, "Cry aloud, spare not, lift up thy voice like a trumpet, and shew My people their transgression, and the house of Jacob their sins."

John 7:37, "In the last day, that great day of the feast, Jesus stood and cried, saying, If any man thirst, let him come unto Me, and drink."

John 12:44, "Jesus cried and said, He that believeth on Me, believeth not on me, but on Him that sent Me."

Luke 8:8, "And other fell on good ground, and sprang up, and bare fruit an hundredfold. And when He had said these things, He cried, He that hath ears to hear let him hear."

G. Have a good spirit when entering the pulpit

Do not be in a bad mood. You are not fit to be a preacher if you cannot rule your emotions! Proverbs 25:28, 16:32.

Conclusion

God wants to use you. If you are going to be a preacher, aim high! Aim at doing this as well as anything you do in your life.

We do not need preachers or pastors in the ministry who are not called and are not trying to be holy. "Many pastors have destroyed My vineyard...." Jeremiah 12:10.

Review these notes, often and constantly look for better ways to communicate the truths of God. Study, study study. A message from God will be found buried in your study somewhere.

"Preach the word; be instant in season, out of season; reprove, rebuke, exhort with all longsuffering and doctrine." 2 Timothy 4:2.

"If the preaching is of an emotional character, it will affect the feelings, but not the heart and conscience. Such preaching results in no lasting good, but it often wins the hearts of the people and calls out their affections for the man who pleases them. They forget that God has said: 'Cease ye from man, whose breath is in his nostrils.' " – *Testimonies for the Church*, vol. 5, p. 301.

www.ingramcontent.com/pod-product-compliance
Lightning Source LLC
Chambersburg PA
CBHW051405150726
48000CB00003B/1340